Door to Door

POETS OUT LOUD PRIZE WINNERS

Jennifer Clarvoe, *Invisible Tender*, 1999
Julie Sheehan, *Thaw*, 2000

Door to Door

POEMS

ROBERT THOMAS

With an Introduction by
YUSEF KOMUNYAKAA

FORDHAM UNIVERSITY PRESS
New York • 2002

Copyright © 2002 by Fordham University Press

All rights reserved. No part of this publication may be reproduced, stored in a retrieval system, or transmitted in any form or by any means—electronic, mechanical, photocopy, recording, or any other—except for brief quotations in printed reviews, without the prior permission of the publisher.

Library of Congress Cataloging-in-Publication Data

Thomas, Robert, 1951–
   Door to door : poems / Robert Thomas ; with an introduction by Yusef Komunyakaa.— 1st ed.
   p. cm.
   ISBN 0-8232-2233-0 (cloth) — ISBN 0-8232-2234-9 (pbk.)
   I. Title.
PS3620.H64 D66   2002
811'.6—dc21   2002007759

Printed in the United States of America
02 03 04 05 06 5 4 3 2 1
First Edition

For Cheryl

"en cada rama guardas testimonio
de nuestras indelebles primaveras"

> Lord, I'm bound for Black Mountain
>   me and my razor and my gun
> I'm gonna shoot him if he stands still
>   and cut him if he run
>
>   Bessie Smith, "Black Mountain Blues"

> And pardon that thy secrets should be sung
> Even into thine own soft-conchéd ear
>
>   John Keats, "Ode to Psyche"

Contents

Acknowledgments	ix
Introduction	xi
HIDE AND SEEK	1
The Nocturnal Toy Peddler	3
Lullaby	4
Ensenada Wedding	5
Foxfire	8
Weather on the Plateau	9
Orestes Remembers the Sea	10
Tails of Ions and Dust	12
Cleaning the Fish	14
The Blizzard	15
Quarter Past Blue	17
HARD-WIRED ANGELS	19
The Blue Willow Curse	21
Love Spell in Two Parts	22
Bonfire	23
Love and Photosynthesis	24
The Barometer and the Shield	25
Helen Back Home in Sparta	26
Wolf Point	27
December Matinee	29
Daphne's Apology	30
Thérèse	31
SAFE HOUSE	33
The Piano Tuner's Widow	35
Lily	36

Plush Fire	37
Into the Poplar Trees	40
Letter to Emily Dickinson from the Golden Gate	41
Elegy Written on Unlined Paper for Emily Dickinson	42
Iseult of the White Hands	44
Afterlives	46
Wild Onions	48
Changing the Oil	49

KNEES UNDER THE WHEEL — 51

The Stamp Collector	53
The Bluest Days	55
Shopping at Night	57
The Poetry Merchant	58
Why I Am Not a Novelist	60
Vertigo at Sea Level	62
Salamander	63
Eurydice's Song	64
Ars Poetica	65
Film Noir	67

SCIENTIFIC METHOD — 69

Door to Door	71
Thinking about Sex	73
The Ballad of Martin and Geraldine	74
Dido's Closing Argument	76
Colorado	78
The Hypnotist	79
Blue Whale	81
Mayflower	83
Repairing the Hubble Telescope	86
The Man Who Could Not Fly	88

Acknowledgments

I want to thank the following publications, in which some of the poems in this book appeared, some in slightly different form, for the first time:

AGNI	"Lily"
The Antioch Review	"Into the Poplar Trees"
Artful Dodge	"Thérèse"
The Atlantic Monthly	"The Blizzard"
The Cream City Review	"The Poetry Merchant"
FIELD	"The Blue Willow Curse," "Quarter Past Blue"
The Iowa Review	"Wild Onions," "Foxfire"
The Kenyon Review	"Plush Fire"
New England Review	"Film Noir," "Vertigo at Sea Level"
The North American Review	"Thinking about Sex," "Helen Back Home in Sparta"
The Paris Review	"Iseult of the White Hands"
Poetry Northwest	"Dido's Closing Argument," "The Nocturnal Toy Peddler"
Puerto del Sol	"Eurydice's Song," "Love Spell in Two Parts"
Seneca Review	"Wolf Point"
The Sewanee Review	"The Man Who Could Not Fly," "Bonfire"
The Southern Review	"Door to Door"
Witness	"The Hypnotist"
The Yale Review	"December Matinee"

I want to thank the members of my writers' group for years of encouragement, insightful criticism, and friendship: Beverly Burch, Nancy Taylor Everett, Grace Grafton, Scott Reid, Zack Rogow, Jeanne Wagner, Jami Wolf, Judy Wyatt, Andrena Zawinski, and especially Diane Kirsten-Martin. Each of them has rescued me from corny or hackneyed lines and, more importantly, from discarding lines worth saving.

I also want to thank the Warren Wilson College Program for Writers. Many poets have been generous in sharing their thoughts, insight, and taste, but in particular Carl Dennis, Roger Fanning, Tony Hoagland, and Laura Kasischke have given of themselves to me more than any sane person could be expected to give.

Finally, I want to thank Cheryl Morris, my wife, for her encouragement, patience, and love, and her always discriminating critical ear for the genuine and the fake. The quotation on the dedication page is from Pablo Neruda's "Every Day, Matilde" ("in every branch you bear witness to our indelible springtimes," *The Sea and the Bells,* trans. William O'Daly [Port Townsend, Wash.: Copper Canyon Press: 2002]).

INTRODUCTION

Yusef Komunyakaa

Robert Thomas's *Door to Door* beckons the reader to enter worlds of surprising poignancy in a time of the cultivated glib. The imagery is original and surefooted, and the book's pacing is almost mathematical, moving with controlled ease. Many small doors can spring open in a single poem; he ushers us through doors that defy bafflement and orchestrated confusion. Realism and surrealism merge in some of Thomas's most striking poems, where two or more worlds collide softly—a tableau of twists and turns that always bring the reader to a door where one is invited to see oneself.

The first poem, "The Nocturnal Toy Peddler," creates a tune that engages the reader's heart and mind:

> Sometimes you hear him in the distance, the tin bells of his cart
> waking you, his voice hawking in Slavic or Illyrian. Who are his
> customers? The children are in bed. Perhaps a mother
>   unprepared
> for next morning's birthday, or the father of a child who has
>   died,
> looking for a pinwheel or wooden train to set on a grave? . . .

This sounds like a very old story told in a new voice. And the folkloric tune of "The Nocturnal Toy Peddler" is even more meaningful in the poem's last lines:

> I pick up a black scissors from his tray, but don't know
> what to do with it. He takes it back, cuts through the skin
> of his wrist as if it were a leather pouch. Gold coins pour
> to the ground. He laughs again. *Don't you know
> your own father? Enough of this craft. Take me home.*

This poet knows how to cast a spell through an unembellished language that propels and recasts the ordinary into the mysterious. The naming of things seems important to Thomas; but the ritual of naming is also deceptive because ordinary objects assume a mythic presence.

Even silence grows tangible and seeks a certain materiality in Thomas's poetry. The unsaid tells everything. In another poet's hands the silence may appear as an emotional shorthand, but poem after poem in *Door to Door* creates a levity we can trust. Look at what he does in "Wild Onions":

> I could write a poem that no one could tell was for you,
> or for anyone. It would just be about the doors,
> the old glass doorknobs in my apartment,
> and Mission Carmel—the rickety stairs
> dense with pigeons all the way up the sealed bell tower;
> the brown fountains, dry but overrun with geraniums;
> and the cemetery with its smell of wild onions,
> irregular stones in adobe shade for two centuries,
> and stray white cats—it would be
> about a silver candlesnuffer
> and a windmill turning in the rain.

Pure metaphor drives this collection. In fact, a poem seems like a small galaxy of metaphors, one touching the other to create tension. Thomas lets us in on the book's overall conceit in the first stanza of "Vertigo at Sea Level":

> The apricot jam on my toast: that, too,
> is metaphor. I mean the thing itself, not
> these words. I mean the moisture
> condensing on my glasses as I walk the ten steps
> from my house to the garage. The heavy door
> opening on its chains. I mean the morning
> and its crates of light unloaded from the cargo hold
> and stacked higher and higher on the dock
> till darkness is only visible through the cracks.

This voice makes us realize that poets are indeed our philosophers, spurring us on to see into the essence of things, to question the very existence of human reality and perception, and to remind us that language itself is a body of symbols that *"means so much more than it is."*

Often, in a Robert Thomas poem, we are in this world and outside it. The ordinary and the fantastic are one. Why are we attracted to such an imagination? Maybe it has as much to do with what we find in these last ten lines in "The Man Who Could Not Fly":

> They have forgotten everything but the lashing wind,
> the occasional glint of a fish far below, and the glare
> as they dive toward the sun. I take off my shirt,
> and my huge, unwieldy wings slowly unfold
> and compose themselves. Heavy as armor,
> they hang useless and serene. Why must I
> come day after day to watch those appalling
> plunges, that awful hovering, the ecstatic
> shrieking wheels while I stand in the dusk,
> my iridescent plumage dignified and rigid?

If these poems at times seem surreal, it is surrealism with a compelling voice, not as an embodiment of linguistic or imagistic tomfoolery, but as a way of unveiling mystery that redeems. When following the twists and turns through *Door to Door*, the reader knows that the two last lines of "The Ballad of Martin and Geraldine" are truly earned:

> Let's scorch the orchid with all our art.
> Take on my bare, unfurnished heart.

Hide and Seek

The Nocturnal Toy Peddler

Sometimes you hear him in the distance, the tin bells of his cart
waking you, his voice hawking in Slavic or Illyrian. Who are his
customers? The children are in bed. Perhaps a mother
     unprepared
for next morning's birthday, or the father of a child who has
     died,
looking for a pinwheel or wooden train to set on a grave? Tonight
I've had enough. The streets are deserted except for pots of blue
lobelia on balconies, and taxis cruising the avenues, masters
of the night. I follow the voice and a ratcheting sound like
the propeller of a toy plane, until I round a corner and see him,
wheeling his cart through a dark playground. There are ribbons
on the spokes, and a mask turning on each hub. My mother's
     face,
speaking to me: *I want you to know, I was happy once, before you
were born, a girl in a lake, water streaming from my ponytail.*
The peddler breaks the spell, asks what I want. I tell him
I came to look, but again he demands, *What do you want?*
The stars in a box, I tell him, buzzing like bugs.
He pulls out a machine that looks like a coffee grinder,
and he points to the crank. As I turn it there are loud skirls
from the drawer. Whale songs. When I open it a white
moth flies in my face and into the night; the old man laughs.
I pick up a black scissors from his tray, but don't know
what to do with it. He takes it back, cuts through the skin
of his wrist as if it were a leather pouch. Gold coins pour
to the ground. He laughs again. *Don't you know
your own father? Enough of this craft. Take me home.*

Lullaby

I lose count of the snowflakes in my bedroom. *Pretty ponies,*
my father sings as he melts. I pad through grizzly white grass.
This must be what they call a blue moon, it makes everything
look as if it's immersed in a mirror. I search for the blue house
I know exists, where the father and mother close the door
to their room and then play hide-and-seek without the "it":
take off their clothes, fold them, and swim without water.
When the door opens, the wood floor is covered with snow.

Ensenada Wedding

It was just across the border.
Your father and I had a pitcher of martinis,
the drink back then (I hear it's back), and we competed
with our friends—the best expression
for a dry martini: I want it
so dry a scorpion would feel at home
basking on the olive.

Of course I insisted on separate rooms: in those days
people drank so hard and danced so soft
they hardly thought of sex. But the next morning your father
had on a starched shirt and navy blue tie,
and a coat despite the heat, when he picked me up
for breakfast. He was so tall
we didn't have to wait when he hailed a cab. He took me straight
to *Iglesia de San Juan de la Cruz*. I'd never seen
streets like that: our cab was bigger
than some of those hovels,
and I remember the smell of the meat.

When we got there the church surprised me: hand-painted
stations of the cross, incense, the red candle hung from the
    rafters
advertising God's presence like a barker—
I almost could have drunk the holy water.
Of course I knew your father
had paid off the priest: he had to—he was divorced.
Enough pesos, the father said, that the church could get a new
    roof.

He knew right away he shouldn't have mentioned the money
in front of me. I had my hair in a French twist
and wore a milk-white suit.

While we waited for the priest to fetch his housecleaner
and her eight-year-old granddaughter to witness,
a cloudburst came out of nowhere; it sounded as if
the whole town were hurling stones against the blue stained
   glass.
That was the closest I ever felt to him.

Our room overlooked the plaza, children hawking
pinwheels and wooden dolls
for tourists to bring home to their children.
I loved him for the wrong reasons,
and I wish that weren't
the definition of love itself, but it is.
He was so handsome in his captain's uniform,
those medals like candy
brimming over the cut-glass bowl of his heart.

I always knew the latest rage,
the mambo or cha-cha, and I'd stay out
as late as I pleased even after you were born—
that you love. Life is strange. It's always seemed best
in high, high heels, with a gentleman who knows how to dance,
no matter his conduct at home.
He had the maid plait bougainvillea vines around our bed
(even now it sounds strange
to say *our*), a different color for each post:
scarlet, coral, apricot, and mauve.
It was stunning,
though not quite enough for me to bear
someone looking at my body
as anything but the carry-on bag
packed with necessities
it had always been for me. What I remember
is the hotel pool the next morning,
swimming in gardenias.

Your father and I had gone through the war.
Bodies meant something
different then, bodies in the dark. All I wanted,
all I want, is *noise*. All that has ever left me
satisfied is a mariachi band
outside my window, burnished trumpets
blaring like taxi horns, the yellow braids
on the guitarists' jackets
twisting tighter as they cry to me from the loud, crowded street
    below,
Canta y no llores, Sing don't weep,
which is what I've always done.

Foxfire

God is my secret; he knows I'm his girl. You don't
know what he's like. Sometimes he licks my face
like a cat lapping cream. I almost caught him once,
but he disappeared down the bole of an oak.
I know he loves me because he gives me presents.
I found a bottle cap once, Red Fox Root Beer,
on the path I take through the aspens. You've never
seen it in a store, have you? A sign clear as candy.
And a bar of soap by a bend in the river, scented
with Rome apples and never used. I bathed with it
for a month, my evening prayer, till it was gone:
God wants his gifts used. The suds down my leg
like apple blossoms on a branch in the dark.
You say he's not real? As soon tell a mother
the child's not real that suckles at her breast.
I stayed with him all night when he had a fever,
fed him shards of ice to keep him alive, and when
I had no water, I cooled him with my own spit
till I couldn't swallow. Who are you to judge?
Come out and you might see something—foxfire
from the rot of a fallen cedar: he's mine.

Weather on the Plateau

Your poem is so different from mine: cowboys and
Air Force pilots, dust, weather on the plateau. How
you did it with your brother when you were children,
but you were a year older and felt guilty. His penis
not a boy's but not yet a man's, both hard and soft
as if made out of soap. Your poem does not forgive
yourself or others. You write of your great-grandfather,
eyes like shrapnel, what he did to your grandmother,
what she did to your father, and what he did to you.
Your poem is about your body, as if you can't see yourself
in the mirror, but must discover yourself part by part,
the smell of the skin of your arm like salty butter.
Even God is mad in your poem, his right eye burned out
long ago, by a saint with a torch, and your universe
fits in the hole he scrapes and claws to ease his pain.

Your poem is about colors I can't see, the ultraviolet
undertow of love, how it hurt so much when your father
looked at you with hate because you couldn't save him,
being neither a boy nor a woman. Your poem is *faster*
than mine, hurtling from Joshua trees to the first time
you stole a book, learned to whistle, had an orgasm
alone on the back porch watching the August fireflies,
listening to Smokey Robinson sing "The Tracks of My Tears"
after everyone had gone to bed. At the end of the song
the melody's so strong it can't be stanched. He didn't need
to sing it anymore, just sketched it with a few notes and let
the brush of dusk finish what the hand and throat began.

Orestes Remembers the Sea

What I remember best is her last bath: already a woman,
she wasn't allowed to wash herself. They fanned the wetness
from her pink scapulas with black-edged palm fronds
scorched by summer. I was a child. They counted on me
not to understand. I did not know what Iphigenia knew,
but I knew *that* she knew, and that was enough.
She knew her father had bartered her blood
for one good west wind to get him off to war.
Our father, who splashed with us in the skittish sea
and sang to us of kites, who fed us apple gobbets
he'd dredged in honey and pierced with his knife.

For ten years our mother plotted. She never
let us forget. Every drop of olive oil
drizzled on our bread was a shrine to our sister.
Each night we sprinkled salt on our pillows
in her memory. And every morning our mother
sliced the figs in silent rage. *We* were *her* sacrifice.
At least *he* picked his darling, the one he loved best,
to clean and to slit. That wine ran into the crevices
of granite, deeper than the pines' roots,
to the very throat of the god. There was nothing
left to bury. We were the dregs.

After ten years of slaughter he strolled in to a feast of lamb
in a rosemary crust. His wife had been preparing the lemon
marinade since the day he left, when the wind rose so tender
he recognized war's voice, shy and irresistible as a child's
invitation to play under the cedar tree in the far garden.

We braided her hair and hung lavender so she slept.
She should have left him to us. Now we had no other
wine to pour but hers. Once, I'd been a boy who dove
and found the indigo shells off the coral reef, the ones
that made the indelible dye, but now the time for rituals
was gone, and would not return with its long blue robes.

Tails of Ions and Dust

I can't even remember our sex life.
What I remember is the fishing village
on the Big Island. Not a tourist
besides the two of us. We averted our eyes
from the cockfight and kicked up red scraps,
firecracker casings from the night before
when we had gotten just drunk enough
to enjoy the presence of a pair of pale green geckos on the wall.

I hurt you so much! And you hurt me, but not
so much. What I remember
is you floating on your back—
it was just after that cult, Heaven's Gate,
killed themselves on a potion of vodka,
phenobarbital, and applesauce
to join the Hale-Bopp Comet,
and we could see it in the sky through the ginger
(I mean through the smell of wild ginger),
and we argued about whether we could see it *moving*.

Not one angelfish brushed my skin
though I knew they were all around my legs
as I supported your back with the tips
of my right hand, a pink starfish.
You were a ridiculously strong swimmer, and I held you
because you wanted to tilt your neck back so far
that you could see it "upside-down"—that's what you said,
upside-down, that's what I can't forget,
your neck tilted back to watch a vapor trail

of coldness and ammonia and CO_2
to see if you could make out
its twin tails, blue and yellow,
and all that ice that came so near the sun
and had not been glimpsed since the Sumerians
baked the mud for the ziggurat of Ur
and went down to bathe in the Euphrates.

Cleaning the Fish

Watering the hedge, I knew what I was doing.
This was before the drought, before everyone
filled their patios with scrubby native plants.
The running waters would quench us forever.

I wrote poem after poem for Jean—sunsets
like gutted trout, that sort of thing (I'd never
cleaned a fish); fuchsias as spiraling flames
(lots of spirals)—I wondered if her husband
read them too. Strapping the cool, abrasive
seat belt over her bare shoulder as we'd go
to the bookstore, she'd get aroused.
I was in heaven, or at least Santa Rosa.
Every once in a while I knew it; mostly I did not.

But the poems went on (nebulas, red noons),
and we fed each other beer and ice cream
on the couch until I saw she wanted to leave
her upholstered home, her wry husband
shoveling snow off the drive before he left
for work, her precocious children, the car
in her garage, and even the folded maps,
and she knew, then, from my fingers' listless
stroke on her lips, that I didn't want her to.

It must have seemed to her that every poem
was a lie, and it was, I see now, it was, though
what I saw flashing in the stream, the rose and
radical flesh, is flashing still—intact, flawless—
in that high country we left behind.

The Blizzard

You'll never take off your blue cashmere
for me, your jade belt, or even your white
walking shoes that squeak like a nurse's.
Whose pulse are you taking now? Why am I
just well enough not to warrant your care?
Those snow-white stockings will never
drift like water lilies on my floor. Instead,
I will row the boat of my sleek, narrow bed
to the center of the lake and bask in the sun,
opening a basket of strawberries, a buttery
cheese, and a musky bottle of Spanish wine,
and very gently, carefully get drunk alone.

I've had the sun's pleasures, but you are the snow
I've never known. I can only imagine the falling
crystals on my tongue, each one the melting word
of a poem in a language I barely know, *fleurs,
chaleurs, douleurs* . . . the blizzard of your body.

Ötzi, the Ice Man, was herding his sheep home
five thousand years ago in the southern Alps, prepared
for anything: a quiver of cherry and dogwood,
a longbow of yew, an ax of burnished copper,
mushrooms and einkorn in a leather pouch,
stripes and crosses of blue-black soot tattooed
on his ankles and back. When the snow came,
he didn't have a chance.

An unusually warm summer, tourists on a picnic,
salami and orange soda in their packs. They saw

the back of his skull jut from the thawing snow
and made a call from a cell phone, talking
excitedly in a language that meant nothing
to Ötzi: strange vowels, inhuman consonants.

If you gave yourself to me for one afternoon,
sunlight lapping at the lace curtains, I'd be lost
in a white storm, no way to find the narrow pass
leading down to the river Adige. I'd lose track
of the whole south, the herd's need for clover.
Look, wrapped in maple leaves and birch bark,
embers I carry from one night's camp to the next,
blow on them, look, still warm, burning my hand
like stinging nettle, its white, fragrant petals . . .

Quarter Past Blue

It's just the sort of paper-thin night
to make me steal the clapper from the mission bell
and leave it on your doorstep like a stuttered prayer.
In your room I see a writing light,
soft and dirty as an oyster.
I know you can hear me
out here in the static,
scraping on your pane like a raccoon.
I've been to the pond.
It's not as if the swans were your personal secret.
Come out and walk with me across the Sonoma
town square, on the edge of the green.
I'm wearing my papier-mâché wings,
and they're not yet dry. The moon's been released
on its own recognizance. This is serious traffic, gridlock
intergalactical, Friday-night lust and spleen. This is
the *it* they mean when they say *this is it*. You are so
caught up in your own devotions. You are so not
what you think you are. It's late,
half past revelation, quarter past blue,
and you're still counting the chits, waiting for something
better than love as cold and magical as dry ice
to come along and sideswipe you, hit and run,
without leaving a scratch.

Hard-Wired Angels

The Blue Willow Curse

You and your Pavarotti carols, your four-wheel drive,
heading through the snow to Aunt Marcella's,
aren't you ever satisfied? Do you need a retinue
of angels, hard-wired? You're so preoccupied,
thinking of the imminent novena for Our Lady
of Kansas City, Our Lady of Baby Back Ribs,
planning your side dish. Isn't there enough
hunger in your own backyard, wiping his boots
on the welcome mat, saddle-soaping his hands?
Yes, Ma'am, don't mind if I do. You can't get
enough, can you, of his knuckles bruised
on the hardware, of his manners of rust.

May a twisted wind blow every saucer and bowl
of blue willowware from its shelf on your hutch
until you eat from an iron pan. May the pan melt
on a forgotten burner and the smell fill your house
while you dream of black rain and your house burns
so that every photograph of your mother and father,
all evidence of their dire existence and the existence
of the elm that overhung their porch and every moth
that fluttered on their screen at dusk, every postcard
every thank-you note from a niece every love letter
from a soldier or hack or taxidermist or perfect fool
is ash and every particle of ash is alone,
in a shimmering hush you'll never know.

Love Spell in Two Parts

Gather a fist of cowrie shells under the wharf. Grind it
into powder and then paste. Smudge a gritty, glittering
dab of this gruel on spots your beloved passes during
her day: the poster at her bus stop, the steps that lead
to her small Victorian flat on Parker Street, the threshold
of the deli where she gets her slaw. She will start to feel
something tugging at her, like a tide, wherever she goes.
She will see gulfweed and golden anemones in the street.

Practice an instrument until you forget her.
She will hear the longing in the syrinx' reeds
gathered from the marsh, the helicon's fire.
The viola d'amore's sonnet of fourteen strings
will win her. She will want the nagara, furious
drums tattooed all night at Hindu weddings.
When she hears the bamboo saxophone
of Sugarbelly at the Glass Bucket Club
in Kingston, her joy will be complete.
You will no longer care about your own.

Bonfire

I scavenge the desert for branches broken from your beloved
Joshua trees, risk picking a few yucca spikes. At flea markets
I find glass vials, lime and rose, that shoot wonderful colors
as they melt. You'd love the old books: some novels are logs—
The Gulag Archipelago takes forever to catch. Each year
I try to top the last. Two years ago I found a beautiful Impala
low-rider with white leather bucket seats and the Holy Family
on the dash. I had to save all year to get it for you.
First I cruised through town, imagining you by my side,
showing off the shocks' shimmy, then parked on my lawn,
took down the hood, piled the seats with the year's loot
and lit a match. Last year the centerpiece was a grand piano.
I even recorded it, the hard wood buckling, the sharp twang
as strings broke, the ivory's sizzle. No one loves you like I do.
This year I'm taking a different approach—set fire to fire.
I've got a thousand candles: Christmas and Hanukkah
and pagan jacks-o'-lantern, candles small as snowflakes
and big as tree stumps, some in a crystal chandelier
hung from a pine tree, some in paper boats, and some
borne aloft on silk kites. I will light them one by one.
Then I'll turn on the gas-primed sprinklers full blast.
One year I will be the tallow, scented with lemon
and Carolina jasmine; the next, I will be the wick.

Love and Photosynthesis

By the time I was sixty miles from your door, my sedan had turned into a low-rider. I was reborn, a gold rosary hanging from my rearview mirror.

I learned something today over the radio, driving through Santa Cruz. Leaves don't turn gold or anything else in the fall. It's the loss of chlorophyll. The reds and violets there all year long become visible, no longer eclipsed by the pagan green. Most of the time we are in a darkroom looking at the negative of what is. Listening to salsa, I passed the mission and saw Mary's statue at the gate, her blue cape weathered to white. Your blue shoes absorb all the colors of the spectrum but one. Only blue is reflected back to our eyes, where it presents itself as the shoes' true color, as if the only true Christians were the ones locked out at the church door. Once love was a blue shoe on the side of the road. I tried to leave you, but I didn't try very hard.

I drove down the highway past Salinas and saw cottonwoods beside a run-down truck stop, out of business—leaves orange as a Baltimore oriole, yellow as a Nashville warbler. I glanced through the window at the rusted cash register and imagined the carousel of mirrors that spun pies of apricot and meringue. I heard a waitress order a Slam Dunk Special, and saw her skeptical, American eyes. I remembered the moment I saw your eyes ante up, deciding you'd take a chance on me, trusting you were just lucky enough to be wrong about everything.

The Barometer and the Shield

The furnace juts from the corridor wall next to us. You ask me if I want some coffee and I follow you into the kitchen, and then I notice your hair, just washed and smelling of vanilla. I cannot even sketch an egg, but for a moment I consider learning to draw so I can paint frescoes on your kitchen wall. Though we have just met, I realize that I want to have a child with you. You slowly swirl the water through the grounds, and a hint of cardamom is released. I feel a need for sugar now. I want my coffee thick as molasses with a twist of lemon slicked on the rim.

By the time you pass me the cream, I am deeply in love, but it will never happen, will it, my fennel cake? Life is a war of the barometer and the shield. Most people swear by the shield, but a few perform autopsies on fallen stars, and they work alone. The shield fears them because it has no defense against their knowledge of snow to come, the horrible loss of the horizon. From the perspective of the shield, the barometer sees *around* the horizon, but it is no mystery that time is space, that it is already tomorrow morning at the Taj Mahal, rose petals fallen on the tile. The future is written in the deliberate way you lift the cup to your lips. The paradox is that we both know it, possessing the same instrument for the measurement of fluctuations in the song of songs.

I stir my coffee, and the teaspoon makes a tinkling sound—wind chimes—as I hear our children playing in the other world.

Helen Back Home in Sparta

Was it worth it, King? To go to war for my rakish figure,
sleek as the prow of your cutter? It must have hurt:
to lose me to a boy with pomade in his hair and a taste
for stepping out and sleeping in. All I missed, Menelaus,
in ten years was the snout of your dog, but now I am home,
husband, my brazen locks unlocked for good. Take a good
gander. By the way, did we have children? I can't remember.

This morning I went out beyond the olive grove,
scrabbled up some rocks and lay with she-goats
who nibbled on lavender in the sun until I slept.
Did you think a swineherd's gossip would amuse me?
I'll never say no. I'll never be too old for Dionysus' lyre.

So you paraded home, dragging your loot, the bronze visor
of the hoplite you killed—a spook on the mantel your gang
and you take turns trying on when you've had too much hooch.
Look at me, Menelaus. I don't know what it is to be armored.
One night I stood on the ramparts of Troy, the whole place
on fire, a thicket of spears making a racket in the sky. All I wore
was a black gown and coronet of pearls. Some hero next to me
got pierced by a spear, and hung like a hog from the bulwark;
I had to tug out the iron from deep in the oak to release him.
I went down to the courtyard, strolled through ten thousand
men at war as if I were at a ball. Not one of them knew me,
but unlike you, unlike you, they knew I was no man's wife.

Wolf Point

I hear the crunch of green spikes
as I walk through the fog, the whole field
covered with ice plant at Wolf Point.
The raucous welter of the ocean
sounds like a helicopter through the mist
churning up a galaxy of salt and foam.
I can't hear you. I didn't know
it would be this cold. Black skimmers
are gliding over the water, I know it,
their red bills scooping up herring
all night long. A hundred years ago a timber wolf
minding his own business surprised a man here
minding his. He had that look of a thing
that's never gotten over being born,
come straight out of nowhere, or the sea,
eyes with the faint pink sheen of the dearest pearls.
The moon melted on his tongue like a gob of fat
as the fire burned, and when he'd had his fill
he turned back to his rift in the black quartz
and was swallowed whole. The man clawed the embers.
Where are you? Did you stay back in the meadow,
nothing but crushed grass and the scent of rosemary?
I can't believe it. With your all-purpose curse
kept so close to your lips night and day, night and day,
and the brazen shoes you'd wear even to the cusp of sunrise,
red heels struck on rock as a dare.
The way you toyed with the white fruit
of the wolfberry, wondering if it were poison. Well,
it's not. I know you: a cypress on the point,

its branches wrenched open by the wind,
and tiny needles fused in clumps dense as shrapnel
in a grenade, ready to explode its own body
just to take with it the vile, ravishing dawn.

December Matinee

You ordered something Russian because you loved sour cream
and wanted to taste caviar. Sepia prints of San Francisco
on the back wall: workmen with ponderous mustaches
laying rail for trolley cars, playing cards
in barbershops, or standing in front of a bank.
We had the restaurant to ourselves,
all the green velvet and brass trim. Please,
I just want to write it down—not all of it
but at least the glint of winter sun
gouging a track across the sky like the sharp runner
of a skate and the sound of the wind honing
its edge on the dark whetstone of the fountain;
the poplar tree in front of the opera house;
the openness of the creamed and powdered
woman in sable who gazes at you as if
she were seeing herself forty winters
before, as if until this moment she had never known
how beautiful she had been; and the flourish of dew
still on the grass as we wait for the men in black
to open the heavy glass doors.

Daphne's Apology

It's better this way. Unable to hold me,
you went back to the work of the sun,
and now I'm a laurel in this metropolis,
watching the old Italian men
betting at pinochle on a park bench,
and the Chinese women
practicing tai chi. Apollo, your heat still turns
my cells to sugar, but my limbs are strong,
black lightning hurled at the clouds.
Girls envy the scent of my crushed leaf.
I still long for your fingers to lift
the small of my back, your breath
on my eyelids, I who will never
sleep again. But I am myself now,
I'm in my element, and I listen
at night to all that stirs: the *corroo*
of a rock dove in Washington Square,
the Cajun music from the radio
in a girl's flat above Caffe Graffeo.
I'm sorry for nothing. The chicory blue
of spring nights runs through my veins.

Thérèse

A whole room full of the Word:
it smelled like my sister's breath
when she'd sneak a smoke behind her locked bedroom door.
My father's congregation did not invite children into its pews,
so they kept me in a back room with the yellow books
drab as the clover on the Oregon pastures
where he'd brought me to look among pear trees
for his grandparents' graves. It was so hot,
and I was so tired—the dust had settled in place
like the parlor where we'd visited my great-aunt—
that I wanted to go home, to the church with moist niches
where holy water was imbued with the scent of the iron
font it had lain in, I thought, for centuries,
and one could put a coin in a rusted slot
to light a red candle that would still be burning
when the plaster-of-paris form of the French girl,
Thérèse, in the vestibule, was rumored to weep
at three in the morning with a gasping joy
down the rough black folds of her dress,
the petals of blue cornflowers on her neck . . .

SAFE HOUSE

The Piano Tuner's Widow

They know me at the flower market.
I get there at dawn while they're unloading the trucks
to pick out the laciest lilies and most violet
gladioli. Whose dirt
shall I decorate today? All I can say for sure
is that it will be no one's I know. It's fun
when they're fresh: imagine the piano tuner's widow
visiting her husband's grave, finding a bouquet
sprawled on the grass like a mistress—
who dared? Who listened with love to his soft hammering
until he found it, the sound he was after? Who watched him oil
the damper and jack?
Sometimes I observe from a colonnade
as someone visits a stone I've festooned.
Sometimes I place a mirror
that just covers the headstone, and books
are a nice touch too: a dog-eared *Turn of the Screw*
or *Catch-22* spurs a double
take from the most oblivious mourner.

I know what you're thinking, but before you judge,
consider this. Aren't I giving them
just what they want, both the living and the dead? Don't you
want to be a mystery when you're gone, a legend?
Don't you want me to wonder where you were all morning—
crossing the Richmond Bridge, driving
toward the Delta, not stopping for whiskey or water?
Yes, it will hurt, but not as much as wasting my life
loving someone who has no secrets,
no safe house or after-hours dive at the river's edge.

Lily

Across the Potomac River, in Arlington Cemetery,
white-jacketed chemists measure the stones,
which go on diminishing, the austere words
etched in gothic bearing the erosion
of the cold purgatory of acid rain.
Each stone is a white hymnal
lifted high by a fundamentalist choir
to hide their frightened faces. The best
times at St. Theresa's morning Mass
were when the people stood for the Last Gospel
and I could curl on the pew
between my mother's legs and the soft, cider-colored wood
and think of a girl with cropped red hair
floating down the street on roller skates
while the priest intoned, "The Word was made flesh,
and dwelt among us." Where is she?
Does she still have legs good for kicking
like the dickens at stars and tin cans (the morning star
was once a can gouged open
full of a girl's piss and ginger beer
before she sent it there)? And my wife, too, likes to buck
and wing it in her flounced dress.
She is one of the kneeling ones working a micrometer,
the exacting tongue of an insect probing the spathe
of the calla
of the candied tomb,
like a dentist gauging the extent of corrosion
of the most beautiful tooth in the world.

Plush Fire

1

It was in the Uffizi Gallery,
the restored painting of a royal Christ
circled by courtiers, not a remarkable work till the original
colors had been bared by acid and scalpel,
the deep greens and reds of the velvet robes,
the intense silence of the golds (the sound of a great bell no
 longer
ringing), the souls both enveloped and expressed by the fabric,
like a Joan of Arc within her plush fire.
When I went out the doors into the humid
city heat, dust clogging the engines of cars on the cobbled streets,
dulling the vendors' souvenirs on the footbridge
over the Arno, the melon and tamarind ice,
I knew that if you had been there, you would have been
too guilty and excited to speak, the painting's rose light
stashed in your memory, in the crack between your shoulder
 blades,
as if you'd stolen a silk camisole from a boutique
and couldn't wait to get back to our pensione
to try it on in the long mirror:
you'd want it all for yourself.

2

It was the only beauty beyond the grasp of Venus,
that of the underworld, so she sent the girl to get it for her,
and Psyche did as she was told. The metallic taste

stung her tongue as she bit the coins
to bribe the old man. She made him take them from her lips,
and smelled the river on his hands. Her beauty
meant nothing here. When he saw the flint
in her eyes he hacked and spit in the water.

When she refused the feast, the candied jellies,
as she had to, and said what she had come for,
the pale queen went and filled the casket with perfume,
and Psyche took it and left,
careful not to slip on the slick rock
as she worked her way back. And the oarsman
kept to himself on their return
to let her know that to him it was only business.
It was after she had gone through all that
and stood gasping under the lemon trees
that she understood what she had to do
and opened the vial she had brought for the goddess
and poured it on her own temples and breasts.

It was hard to tell how long she had lain there
when he found her at the edge of the orchard,
cold and pale as a mirror. And it was no kiss
that woke her, but the quick, surgical
slur of his arrow (its gold barbs
cast in his stepfather's forge, its shaft fletched
by his father's gray hands—how could he
have known its true source, and whose will
he had worked out?) in her mortal veins.

3

You've never been out of America, but that paradoxical
desire of yours to promenade on cloistered streets,
staring ahead while all the eyes peer down on you
from hidden sitting rooms, is so European,
so cynical and yet sentimental, as if you knew

you'd never get what was yours unless you stole it:
and you were right, all that cruel artifice
had to be, the ornate lies, the porcelain jug
and water glass on the marble stand
next to the bed in that tile-floor room,
you had to keep it all to yourself,
because of what you knew—that beauty
is a humiliating, little object
like an artificial kidney you need to carry in an awkward
metal case wherever you go—that there was more truth
in one thread of Christ's painted robe
than in any actual blood, and you'd burn layer
on calcified layer to get at it,
as Psyche lit the forbidden lamp
and shone it on Eros' curls and then watched
as the hot oil hissed and fell on his skin
and he woke and fled
back into the stunned, star-plundered dark.

Into the Poplar Trees

There are no mailboxes on the side of the highway
at Loveland Pass, Colorado, shagged by snow.
The moon is so smooth in the twilight! Why did we stop
just here? The car idles as you walk away
into the poplar trees for no earthly
reason. I light a cigarette, for once in my life,
out of the crisp gold pack you've left on the dash
and watch the smoke smudge some flakes of snow
before they vanish. This blackstrap shit
tastes like God's exhaust if he were a diesel truck
accelerating past me on the road to Denver,
headlights filling my rearview mirror,
horn blaring, then fading to a whippoorwill
that vanishes in a ragged tuft of spruce, the ember's
hiss on my lips. I'm so tired as I pace
the ice crust on the tar that when it cracks
I start to shield myself from the stars.
There's nothing to lean on. Ann,
I want to be a white stone
in the snow so you will love me. I want to be
a white-antlered elk that's never sniffed
the heady, sour-mash smell of human skin
so you will come back. I want
to be the exposed white throat of winter
offering itself to the distant, shimmering
fangs of one of its own kind.

Letter to Emily Dickinson from the Golden Gate

You would have loved the Pacific,
the whole damn sky a hummingbird's
throat. The iridescence
as an abalone shell cracks open
on the otter's breast.

A tumbler of sherry at a corner table
on the Barbary Coast: I would have shown you
a good time. We could have had ourselves
a real conversation, Keats and peach cobbler
and the Lincoln-Douglas slavery debates,
whose acid grace had burned a swath from Illinois to Amherst
and the San Francisco piers. Nothing
would have shocked you, a few strands
of your chestnut hair loosening
in its pins as you met the linen merchant.

But you had known more of the intervals
and octaves of heaven in your drawing room
than I could show you in any honky-tonk
or sumptuous opera house, and more of hell
in your church with lilies all over its cross.
I would have had nothing to match
the white force of your mind's furnace
as you hiked your skirt to board the train
scorching home.

Elegy Written on Unlined Paper for Emily Dickinson

She composed her own funeral with a rigor
that rivaled the geometry of her azalea beds,
and wouldn't let anyone haul her to the First
Congregational Church on a lurching wagon,
but ordered her body borne on the shoulders of six men
straight through the barn and back field
to the West Street Cemetery. They lowered her gently
to rest in a cradle of pine boughs
as she had lowered gingerbread and cherry jam
in a wicker basket
to a pair of angels beneath her window.
She studied botany in school,
and was the only one to sit stiff on her straight-back chair
when the headmistress asked all to rise
who would be Christians.
Did her father understand,
that stern attorney who once, story has it,
broke into the chapel at dusk to toll the bronze bell
to alert all Amherst to a sunset
he found remarkable?
Her life was scored by one death after another
and once by a more personal scar—
when the eye doctor told her
for six months she must not read or write,
and the fascicles of blue-ruled paper
that she stitched by hand
lay in her desk.
It was May 15, and she lived on Main Street,

in a house with a white fence and a veranda
overlooking a hawthorn and a walnut tree
and a sunrise so intense it could only be seen through a lens of
  debauched
lilac shadows.

Iseult of the White Hands

1

They called me that because of how I sew,
quick as mercury still, at my age;
the threads leap through silk like dolphins
through water, and I remember the sails.
Whatever they said, I never loved him,
not even when he smeared the blood
on my lace garments and I had to gasp
at how he knew what I wanted and hid it
and took my waist and led me to the table
of our drunken guests; not when awakened
by the acrid smell in the air I found him
standing on the balcony staring at nothing,
not even the deranged sky, as indifferent
to *seeing* as an ash tree struck by lightning,
a silhouette against the fields of barley;
not when he rode the cliffs so hard
I thought the earth would quench him
if it dared. If they thought I cared
about *her* they understood nothing.

2

It was as though he could feel her very breath
warming his nape, but it was the morning
entering the chapel nave through stained glass
as he knelt, asking for nothing. He never told me;

I knew. The light was viridian and Paris blue.
Outside the king's men lit the fagots for him—
the sweet aroma—and he remembered the scent
of sandal and quince she had worn belowdecks.

Afterlives

In one, I am reading you a Spanish mystery about a game of chess, and you are reading me a biography of Catherine of Aragon, the first wife of Henry VIII, falsely believed at the time of her death to have been poisoned with Welsh beer. We can follow both plots of our duet at once: it's as easy as driving a mud-spattered pickup through a forest while listening to bluegrass on the radio.

In another, I am buying you a churro on the Santa Cruz boardwalk, cinnamon and sugar coarse as sand in the grooves of crisp dough, but you have wandered off from the churrería. The Pacific Ocean shrinks to a dime on a parking lot, not enough to be worth stooping to pick up and pocket. Later we look over the railing at the serrano red sunset and lick salt from our lips.

In one we can hear the ocean from our bedroom in Cincinnati.

In another we are nocturnal. Sometimes we go out at noon and see a dog asleep on the warm stone steps of the post office, people veering around him as they rush to buy stamps on their lunch hour, and it is as strange as an orange tree at midnight.

In one our daughter is an abstract expressionist who works in blue and orange. We wonder about her sex life. It must be intense, unsentimental. Her paintings are abstract but clearly *interiors*, with forms suggestive of doors and mirrors ajar.

In one, you're driving your Mercury across the desert toward Las Vegas, where you've always wanted to go. You've timed it to arrive at night so you can see the sizzle of lights in the distance. The car's never lost its good-luck shimmy, and you've got the radio turned on as loud as it gets. You want to have a good time and dance like a dune buggy. You want to burn money the way a welder burns acetylene. You want to kill the son of a bitch who never warned you it would hurt like this.

In one I am alone, riding a bicycle around a reservoir, watching a deer stoop to drink, her wet hooves glistening as she glances back toward her meadow. I ride with a perfect balance I was never able to maintain in life, now that it is meaningless, and remember when I rode so fast I could not make a turn and careened into a telephone pole and later sat on the stoop, my elbow packed in ice, surrounded by an unruly gang of fireflies in the dusk and knowing I had it good.

Wild Onions

I could write a poem that no one could tell was for you,
or for anyone. It would just be about the doors,
the old glass doorknobs in my apartment,
and Mission Carmel—the rickety stairs
dense with pigeons all the way up the sealed bell tower;
the brown fountains, dry but overrun with geraniums;
and the cemetery with its smell of wild onions,
irregular stones in adobe shade for two centuries,
and stray white cats—it would be
about a silver candlesnuffer
and a windmill turning in the rain.

Changing the Oil

"No it is not the true story.
No you never went on the benched ships.
No you never came to the towers of Troy."

Stesichoros

1

You are not the Virgin of Guadalupe, "River of Wolves,"
who appeared on the hemp cloak of Juan Diego
when he spilled out its burden of winter roses.
When I see you promenade through a field of larkspur,
the blue wildflowers seem sophisticated, ironic, urbane.

2

You are not Barbara Stanwyck, so smart and sexy
in those early films, conning Fonda with a double
Scotch and soda, double-talk and a stacked deck.
You are not the croupier at the roulette wheel
or the blackjack dealer wearing diamond studs
with the pearl-handled revolver in her purse.
Your lips are burned so raw from the scalding brew
you swig from dawn to dusk, it hurts when you kiss.

3

You are not my first love, who set yellow
primroses adrift down her dark river of hair

and loved the power her body had over me,
how she could torment me just by mentioning
she'd played "ponies in the snow" with Margot.
Sometimes when I'm talking to you on the phone
and you're giving me grief, the blue and white
de Kooning slathers of sky outside my window
seem nearer, more vivid, than the sketch of birch
I view them through. You make the real look real.

4

You are not a revelation. You are not the Word.
You read the atlas the way others read the Bible
or Koran, the way I read Proust: Lilongwe
is the capital of Malawi, where the sunrise glides
over Lake Nyasa; Sofia is the capital of Bulgaria,
where the sun staggers blind out of the Black Sea.
You give me chapter and verse; you've made me a convert:
the Ganges flows languorously toward the Bay of Bengal.

5

I never heard your voice in the dew on the threshold.
I never saw your flame in the sheaths of morning.
You make love the way you change the oil
in your Oldsmobile, taking it seriously, keeping track
of what goes where, making sure nothing gets lost, gets
wasted, meticulously turning a delicate socket wrench.
You get drunk on the shine of the crankcase,
the grit of old oil and the satin of new
as you rub it between your fingertips,
and spread your grimy hands beneath the grit of stars.

Knees under the Wheel

The Stamp Collector

When my grandfather pasted the lime and lavender stamps,
from countries that no longer existed, on black vellum sheets,
where were you, God? When he let my father sit on his knee
and brush the glue on the back of some parakeet or queen,
didn't you learn how to rule? When you wove islands for us
in your star-loom, couldn't you once let us work the treadle?

For Christmas I got a chemistry kit from Dad,
a red metal box with a latch like my lunch pail.
Litmus, from a powdered blue lichen that turns
red in acid. Sulfur and salts and small corks.
I never took one shining vial out of the box.
No one showed me how. Dad was rototilling the earth
along Silverado Road to prepare it for the oleanders
that later I loved to water, like a god, with a special nozzle:
sometimes a light rain falleth, sometimes a torrent of wrath.

For the sausage and beans with brown sugar sauce
every Saturday night at my father's house, I thank you,
Lord. For my stepmother, who played cribbage and hearts
with me, taught me how to keep score with wooden pegs,
and told me I had beautiful hands, thank you. Thank you
for the tumblers of Scotch, no water, my grandfather poured
my girlfriend and me when we were seventeen, and for his
    collection,
its mysteries of canceled and uncanceled, hinges and grills.

For a stamp as small as a communion wafer on my tongue,
the *Nymphalidae* butterfly of the Isle of Espiritu Santo,
and the Blue Moon moth of Vanuatu, thank you, Lord.

For the heilala of Tonga, whose petals adorn the neck and hips of dancers till they wilt and give up, shredded and torn, their silent, intimate perfume, I thank you, oh sweet, hard-drinking, hardworking, and merciful Lord.

The Bluest Days

It's Tuesday evening. No, it's Sunday. See, already
I'm caught in a lie. My mother could never understand—
never, perhaps, forgive—how in fourth grade I fell
so in love with Lisa Gander's handwriting
that I traced her crimped scrawl until I had ruined
my own script. When someone I barely knew died,
Annie said he was the kindest man
she'd ever known. I'd seen him nodding once
in the corner of a room, part of a conversation
I couldn't hear. I think of that now
and know Annie was telling the simple truth.
Sometimes I think I've locked the keys in my car
more than any other human being on this earth. Sometimes
birds of paradise drift through the bluest days
on their boat-shaped bracts,
their small blue and orange fore-and-afts
tacking into the wind, and poetry is desire, a quality
it happens to share with most other forms of conversation.
The boy's desire for new shoes with a jagged stripe,
the girl's for chalk (white, satiny chalk!),
lift off with enough force to air condition a thousand homes
in Albuquerque, where I once won a dance contest,
a pitcher of whatever beer they had on tap.
It tasted as if it had slept overnight
in a corner of the cloakroom, and at first
I couldn't even find the girl I'd danced with
to share the prize. She was kind, perhaps
the kindest person I've ever known, as funny
and beautiful as *A Midsummer Night's Dream*,
and when she took me home at five in the morning,

her mother cooked us eggs and sausage
from a pig she'd slaughtered herself. Kindness and lies
and desire. Wanting to be someone else,
someone nodding in a corner in a sugar-white
T-shirt and jeans, talking about Shakespeare
and where to get a decent cup of coffee
and how crucial it is to be able to—
someone nodding at the barn swallows
quietly entering through a forgotten window propped open,
coming to rest on the wooden beams just beyond
the oblivious shoulders of strangers—
nodding at the white markings that must have evolved
into their elegant, lanceolate form
on blue forked tails a few million years ago.

Shopping at Night

Look at the blue iguana, the red porcupine
in the window of the import store, and right next door
the threadbare wedding dress. Look at the photograph
of the rancher and his family on their finca, posing
in their Sunday-morning finery. This is just
the sort of eerie evidence I want you to confront:
proof that love is a seller's market,
a black market that, like God,
knows no circumference.
It would be a mistake for us
even to try to negotiate, as if we could
cut a deal with a pillar of fire.

Look how different the world looks to itself
when the shops are closed. That's all
I mean. And that we have no choice
but *mano a mano* exchange:
you in a pinto-blotch poncho,
blond hair cut curt as a peach, erotic and practical,
me in my lambskin gloves.

Wedges of Gouda in the delicatessen window
smile like a jack-o'-lantern.
Bludgeons of beer
hang peaceful as bats from a bar's dark racks.
Once you've seen
what we've seen, what the rainspout
witnesses from the eaves—the rusted moon
as it rises in the locks—
there's no turning back.

The Poetry Merchant

There is a man in Buenos Aires behind a rosewood desk
who will pay well, very well, I assure you, for a tin ring
stolen from the hand of a man sleeping on the doorsteps
of Manhattan. If I can bring him the street sign
from the alley, it doubles the price. You can make
a good living. If I drive out to the desert and collect
casings from rounds shot at the moon by men drunk
on Fools' Gold beer, if I can get a bottle full of bullets
caked with ash from a desert fire, there are women
excited by the desert who will pay dearly. Best of all
are the children: it is easy to trade a pack of gum
for a lock of singed hair from a girl's ponytail,
and not much harder to get a sample of blood
from a boy's knee skinned on a playground. I open
my satchel, and the pupils of the affluent grow wide,
but they know their business: they know the genuine
from the fake, and what they do to those who try
to deceive them, well, to see it once is enough.
They know they can trust me: when I tell them the water
in the tiny blue cruet is rain from Kashmir that has never
touched the ground, they know that it is not the tears
of the gang member's sister that cost me an hour's
conversation on the fire escape of her family's apartment,
distracted by the pregnant bitch bathing itself in the dirt,
and different from the water I skimmed from a tide pool
in the Galápagos Islands. Once I sold a broken string
from the guitar of a musician who played old country blues
like "Peach Orchard Mama" on the sidewalk of 101st Street

for an exorbitant price to a man with box seats at the opera. Once I sold an hourglass full of fine sand I had scavenged from under swings where children were playing at dusk, too intoxicated to go home.

Why I Am Not a Novelist

Lights come on in apartments above the shop windows as a man talks to himself along Judah Street. He is the narrator of the novel. He orders a hot piroshki from the Russian bakery and devours it before he has gone a block. "Who does she think she is, staring at me from her nail salon? Is it my fault she has no customers? How can I concentrate on my work when I am under constant surveillance?"

The man performs interesting, important work. Though its nature is never revealed, it is crucial to the novel that its significance be credible. Perhaps he is a poet lost in the novel's urban labyrinth, a counterintelligence agent employed by the wind shear. The streetcar tracks are still slick from an earlier rain as he crosses, guilty that his girlfriend will be hurt that he is not bringing anything home for dinner. "Why should I? We have Sunday's soup, kidney beans like rubies in mud and ziti, pasta like the small white eggs of amphibians. Yes, that's it, an amphibian! That's just how I feel. . . ."

A woman across the street is fishing for the keys to her front door while with her other hand she clutches a bag, a pair of baguettes jutting out. Despite her awkwardness, she has such an air of competence that the man imagines spending the night with her. She lives in that romantic foreign country of all people who live alone: the country, no matter how bleak, where people can play their favorite song, "Stella Blue," a hundred times in a row, and turn on their lamp at three in the morning just to see the shadow of the lampshade fall on the wall. How he would love to be there when her fingers come together with a safecracker's finesse to turn the switch, but all he can do is continue his walk to delay for a few minutes his arrival home.

"Our Mother who art on Market Street," he prays, "waiting

for a dryer at the laundromat, hallowed be thy short hair. Help me to fasten the buttons on my coat when my hands are stiff. Help the drivers on all thy trains to stay awake and blow the whistles. Help the cat, let out to piss under the fire escape, find his way home. Give us our salt and our uninsurable shelter. Lead us not onto the third rail. Show us thy window, Mother, behind the rusted shutters. Show us the secret fingering."

A scent of mint haunts the railing as he finally walks up the stairs. When he opens the door, he hears the television in the back room playing strange music, like a Tibetan chant sung by children from North Carolina. For a moment he thinks he has entered the wrong apartment. He must never have noticed before how dark the wood of the wainscoting is down the hall, how blue the strip of wallpaper. This is only the first chapter, but he hears his girlfriend in the back room chanting a high, Appalachian harmony, not knowing yet that he is home, her feet tucked under her ass, junk mail scattered like white petals on the coffee table, and he knows this is the real story, not what happens next. This is what needs to be told.

Vertigo at Sea Level

The apricot jam on my toast: that, too,
is metaphor. I mean the thing itself, not
these words. I mean the moisture
condensing on my glasses as I walk the ten steps
from my house to the garage. The heavy door
opening on its chains. I mean the morning
and its crates of light unloaded from the cargo hold
and stacked higher and higher on the dock
till darkness is only visible through the cracks.

And you, too, with your powder blue shoes and vertigo
making me crazy with desire. How you park
on the tracks and crank up the Pearl Jam.
The mist is really surging now. Here we sit,
dizzy at sea level. And I mean on the rails,
watching the waxwing perched on the track,
the yellow band at the tip of its tail, and the echoing
chrome wings on the hood. It all *means* so much
more than it *is*. Your plaid skirt rests on your lap,
just above the knees, like a salad
you're carrying to a potluck.
We hear a shrill whistle in the distance.
Nothing is quite as erotic, I mean
as metaphoric, as your knees under the wheel.

Salamander

Of course I burned what I wrote.
What did you expect,
Federal Express?
I rigged up a shack of kindling on the andirons,
stroked and poked.
My father used to call it a salamander, the hook he'd use
to prod logs. That's a good word
for me: the lizard
that lives in the blaze.

Sometimes my words come back to me;
not often. This morning
by the Swannanoa River I noticed water striders skating
helter-skelter
across the river, and for no reason at all
I thought *Fat and sassy
tongues of flame*. And as I crossed the bridge, *your blue
bloodshot eyes*. The problem is: once I think of a scrap,
I remember the whole sweetmeat feast.

I lay down on a dune
where someone had had a picnic, a slew of wings
like new driftwood.
Once I was such a beautiful mess even you
fell in love with me. I was an ear of corn, all my silk tassels
intact, and you, such a husker,
such a waterdog.
You never left a mark
as you held me between your teeth.

Eurydice's Song

I'll never forget that afternoon. Where were you then?
I had to get out of the house. The mirrors were sweating,
our home a clay oven: I could feel myself turning to bread.
I headed for the river, the bend where you and I
used to swim, but dragonflies galvanized the air
and the beekeeper saw me. I ran because his hands
were big as honeycombs. I ran because even the sun
oozed a cloying juice. You tell me, Orpheus, you know
everything. Of course I tripped and fell, choked by fumes
of poppies and thyme. Something sharp sank so slowly
into my ankle I didn't know I was hurt. It was a release,
nectar filling me. When I was brim-full it turned into
a thousand bees stinging, like stars coming out inside
my skin, like the brain-hive of a mad, stubborn queen.
Then they stitched shut my eyes for the journey to come.
The next I knew I was on a raft, and after a while the colors
under my eyelids went away. I tried to keep track, determined
to make sense of it. Now I recognized the scent: pomegranate—
we weren't going down river: we were crossing. I thought I
heard voices, but it could have been the water, whispering
over and over its most soothing word, *now, now now*.
You should remember that, Orpheus. That's what real song
has to say, the *now* of the waters, and sometimes the *there,
there there* of the wind. That's what I've learned; it's not
such a mystery. You were warned not to look back:
I would never follow once I saw what was in your eyes.
Bring the living back a song not heard before, not of you
and your quest, not of a fierce wind but the wind *here*,
that lifts no trim ship's sails and follows no loud god,
but moves so gently through cattails that not one reed
shivers as its seed is borne aloft through dark rushes.

Ars Poetica

Coleslaw clogs the kitchen sink. I'm waiting
for the plumber. *Coleslaw:*
one of the great words of the English language,
the sort poets live for. Its perfect music,
plosive and sibilant. Who wants to eat?
My grandmother sliced the cabbages,
purple and green, year after year, her fingers raw and
sometimes bloody, muttering in German
as she dropped walnuts into the steaming
anarchy to cut the sulfurous odor.

No one knows where it comes from.
Stranger than Stonehenge,
its white roots first appeared
to the Celts (who may have invented sauerkraut!),
and Viking longships were stocked with cabbage and vinegar
when they navigated ice floes
all the way to what they did not call the new world
but just the richest fishing ground they'd ever plundered.

I don't have to tell you about the Napoleonic Wars,
how French grenadiers and Russian families endured
and did not endure famine on the outskirts of Moscow,
or the masterpieces of beets, horsemeat, onions
and green, quartered heads boiled by artisans
as anonymous as the sculptors of the gargoyles.

But I must tell you this:
a head of cabbage was in the cauldron
simmering on the fire when a red fox

mounted the porch as nonchalantly as a penitent
climbing the stone steps of a cathedral, confident of forgiveness.

A dusting of caraway
was left on the sill
when the lovers disappeared
with all the sweet carrots.

When a man climbed out of the sea
and began to walk toward the domes of a distant city,
not knowing if he would be recognized,
not knowing if he would recognize
the blue steps, the plum tree and its moan,
wild cabbage was blooming on the rocks.

Film Noir

I look for you everywhere: in the 4:00 A.M. red snapper alleys
of Chinatown, slick of fish on the street with blocks of ice,
men still swilling bowls of hot noodles and onions in silence;
down the aisles of the Basilica of Star of the Sea, votive candles
in the alcove, no sound but the click of my shoes on Spanish tile;
down terraces of lurid azaleas overlooking the bay as the yellow
lights of the bridge come on—but there's not a trace, not a foil
from one of those tamarind treats you suck on all day, not a star
out of place. Did you ever exist? I come back to my room,
a charred pot of water on the stove I forgot to turn off,
and wash my face in the city's hard water. Why go on?
I could talk to a thousand cab drivers, hedge trimmers, and
altar boys—they wouldn't know a thing, not if I gave them
a hundred-dollar bill and asked them to drive down every
doglegged back road on the coast until they remembered
something, anything, unusual: a dowager teaching French
to her cockatiel in the cage on the backseat, *"Enchanté!"*

Was there perhaps a girl in a pink chemise walking down a dirt
road carrying a sextant? No? Then was there perhaps a winter day
without a cloud in the sky? I am looking for any vestige. There are
in fact hopeful signs: I searched the Old Mint, abandoned for years,
and found a lens on the marble floor, a *camera* lens; someone
on my bus left behind a French novel, one of those with the white
paper covers and red lettering: *La Veste verte*, "The Green Jacket";
there is a theater out near Land's End, the Surf, where a handful

of people emerge and disappear in the fog, not wanting to talk.
You went out for a cigarette and silence and never came back,
and I was left with a tartan scarf and your final mot juste:
Only those who love are not afraid to be alone. Whitehorse,
Vera Cruz, Yangzhou: you could be anywhere, anything—
pearl fisher, drag racer, lightning rod. I'd give you up if I could,
but I see a white gardenia reflected in the watchmaker's window
under his awning, and in the corner of my eye a woman zips up
her rose umbrella and goes downstairs to the underground rail.

Scientific Method

Door to Door

I know this suitcase doesn't look like much, but stroke
this leather. That's history. The man who enjoyed this
before me was a legend. He owned a car whose name
you wouldn't know. That's the kind of man he was.
They say the backseat had candles, not a drop of wax
ever touched the walnut no matter how fast he drove
down dirt roads in the pink shade of almond blossoms.

Can I come in? I've got something I want to show you
you won't believe. Shut your eyes. Let me put this crystal
atomizer in your hand. It's heavy but the spray's as soft
as a word of thanks. Tell me where it's taking you.
The first morning of spring thaw, isn't it? I know everything
you've lost. You haven't smelled it since you were a tomboy
in west Pennsylvania. It's the mist: it brings back whatever
you've forgotten. For me it's the smell of the city in January,
dirty slush. For some, old maps and cinnamon pencil dust.
For you it's the Algonquin River, periwinkle on the banks.

There's another item I have to show you: this oval mirror.
Look at yourself: you won't see the same face twice.
Who's that driving a blue pickup down Interstate 29?
Why is she playing that music so loud? Look again.
She's kneeling in a temple, praying to a stone god.
Now she's naked, except for pink sandals. She slips off
one shoe, then another, dances round them as if taunting
a tense partner, daring you to join her, but before you can
she slithers back into the thin straps, makes a few quick
jabbing steps as if stubbing out a cigarette. You look again;

no one's there. When you touch the mirror it shatters;
your arm plunges into the water of an ice-glazed river.

Come outside for a minute and look at the steel-eyed sun.
Look at the skid marks on the clouds. That's how we live.
Look at all the shadows without any source: blue shadows
of migrating birds darkening the butte under an empty sky,
green and blue-green shadows of rain on untouched ground.
You see what the fire sees, what the breath and the blue.
You see what the glacier sees in the onslaught of spring.

Thinking about Sex

The mystery of horns and hair.
I put on my black shoes in the morning. Blues
on the radio, fog burning off the ridge. Don't
you see it? No one promised it would do any good.
Like God, it's everywhere, but it's some places more
than others: it has its tabernacles, its mosques.
You can smell it in old bookstores and new cars.
It likes windows and especially window coverings:
damask curtains, hook-and-slat shutters, Venetian blinds.
It loves black-and-white movies and Mediterranean colors:
Etruscan red, Naples yellow, Alexandrian blue.
It frequents all points of departure: piers, terminals,
lobbies, bus stops. It loiters in hallways and sidewalks,
knowing time is on its side. The redbird perched alone
on the longest branch of a red cedar is full of it.
The apple snail coiled in its pink shell feels it
in its slow breath as it crosses the pond floor.
You can hear it in the song of the diva and the metal-
on-metal shriek of brakes. A woman in a broad-brimmed
hat gets into a taxicab. A man holding a flashlight
walks across a bridge. Don't you see it? A white-masked
woman makes one incision and spares a bank clerk's life.
A man looks through a telescope at a comet that will not
come again in his lifetime. A woman dives into a river.
A man zips shut a suitcase. What are *you* doing?
Climbing the stairs to a room that smells of rose water?
Turning out a brass lamp? All around you clouds are
forming and reforming, blown on a dry Santa Ana.

The Ballad of Martin
and Geraldine

Why don't you pick me one of those hard green
apples off Mr. Flint's tree? You see that branch
sprawling over our shed? I'll bet that juice's tang
would blind a person if it were spit in his eyes.
The ladder's buried in back of the shovels.

I'll do what I can. The sun is surely ripe.
You've got quite a collection of junk here.
Who ever kept what in all these Mason jars?
Even a bridle and reins. Your father never had horses,
did he? Someone around here used to ride.

Hey, you remember that snake skin we found
on the shortcut to town? I'm going to be about that dry
if you don't move. It was a pretty thing, wasn't it,
those red and white bands like peppermint
swirled through black licorice. It was perfect.

There's something leaking through the roof,
and I can't seem to fix it. Sometimes
I wonder what goes on in there.
They put leather blinders on God
to lead him out of the burning barn.

Don't we make a pair. Don't we make
a scientific method. You don't understand.
I can't rain. I can't do simple arithmetic.
We're a suspension bridge in ruins.
Don't we make a tangling of the air.

I wouldn't have it any other way.
Let's put our ears to the iron ground
and see if we can hear the sun
coming toward us like the A train
from the other side of the world.

Let's lurk in the alley where the picture show exit is locked
and the moonlight skulks.
No one but us and the other predators—
chicken hawks and brindled cats—
is awake in this whole town.

The lamppost shadow crossing our path,
and the weathercock shadow that grates
on the church back door. Here, I've got it.
This one's a Christmas ornament.
I can almost feel a pulse underneath its skin.

Toss it here. There are moments one can bear.
Come watch me breathe the air. Oh, take me
on, take off my hand-me-downs.
Let's scorch the orchid with all our art.
Take on my bare, unfurnished heart.

Dido's Closing Argument

1

You look ridiculous in that armor. Your pink flesh
will be poached like salmon. It couldn't hurt
to stay one more day. Your mother gave you that
gold pear you wear round your neck, didn't she,
before she slunk off to Olympus' backstreets.
Let me shine it with my breath and flaxen sash.
Our wedding was witnessed by a dove and a she-wolf.
Where are you off? I'm not a field you can let lie fallow.
My rivers need bridges and my bridges bright chariots.
I want a pride of sphinxes that will make Egypt blanch.
The feral children who scavenge my shores want a king.
Bring me the son we never had and tell him to negotiate
with famished dogs for his dinner because you are busy
massacring a gang of Etruscans dolled up in war paint.
Murderer, liar, fraud—yes, these can be terms of praise,
but I blush at the word I can still only whisper: *coward*.
I gave up my godhead for you—no more than every lover,
but now you talk like some lawyer and say it didn't count
because no slave lit the marriage torch at the foot of our bed?
That morning we raced on the edge of the earth you knew.
You knew. This torrid light has every shade you ever wanted.

2

You don't even recognize me, do you? That smell's not
mustard or mint; it's something that grows in the dark.
I know you've had to slog through blood to get here,

but here every breath is a burden. Not that I miss it,
the sunsets like red meat. But I would like to hear
how the stars are. I'll bet their gears have shifted.
I remember lying in a fennel field and the vertigo
as I looked *down* into swarming summer galaxies.
That's what you have on earth: the freedom to fall.
If you don't know its worth, if you've just come to pay
a visit, save your bright voice for your victory jubilee.
You have nothing to compare with my white orchards.

Colorado

Nina said it reminded her of orgasm—the broken light
rippling the tide on Bodega Bay—an orgasm that hurts,
intense as crushed ice from a cocktail of lime and grenadine
gone straight to the brain. A sunburn had started to bloom
on the arch just above her blue eyes. I asked if she'd drive
to Colorado with me. We could be there in time to see fall,
when the leaves redden as if blood rushed to their surface,
as it does during sex. Stop it, she laughed, I'm as fertile
as those mythical swans that get excited whenever
a zephyr dishevels their feathers. Still, it's something
to think about, I guess. Teal and mandarin red, all the hues
of shot silk spanned the horizon. The fan snapped shut.
It's hopeless, she said, we both know it. Yes, I thought,
we know so much, we're the perfect match. Something
to think about, I said, is more than most people ever have.

The Hypnotist

She taps her pen once on her desk, and the lemon scent
of my grandmother's pancakes in Cedar Grove, Indiana,
is all there is. When she taps twice, I am with Laura
on her parents' porch. She discreetly lifts her T-shirt
and presses her nipples to mine as if pressing a finger
to my lips, while in her brother's room Jimi Hendrix
sets his guitar on fire.

When she taps the third time, I am riding with my father
in his blue Studebaker, going to see his grandparents' graves,
where he wants to lie someday. He seems to be lost as we drive
down the dark lanes of an orchard, going in circles until we run
out of gas. I watch him walk off, awkwardly dipping his tall
    frame
under the apricot-laden branches. An iridescent dragonfly lights
on the side-view mirror, then darts off toward an irrigation ditch.
He never comes back.

The hypnotist snaps her fingers. Her wood floor glistens
as if made of water. A grandfather clock looms over my chair,
but I can't see the time. She says, *Once more.* I tell her no,
I have to go, and I open the car door and step on the moist
soil. Everything's in black and white. I pick a black apricot
and pitch it at the sun, then head out of the grove, the same
direction my father had gone forty years before. There's a silver
glint in the ditch, and I pick it up. I understand it's the key
to the present, but I know it's the lock that will be hard to find.

I see smoke in the distance, a silent farmhouse.
When I get there, a scent of quince fills the porch. A woman

plays Russian solitaire with her back to me at the kitchen table.
Dishes, gray flowers, rattle as I cross the floor, and she turns.
It is the hypnotist, who I now realize is my wife. She leads me
upstairs to a night table, a wooden box: locked, never opened.
There's a white comb in the mirror. I turn the key and it fits.
The box is empty except for the music, and awkwardly
we start to waltz, the white comb in her hair, the song—
from another continent, another century, another weather—
as much our own as the loudest "Red House" or "Purple Haze."

BLUE WHALE

His father worked for the railroad and didn't approve,
so he took a pen name
from a Czech poet he admired:
Neruda. A locomotive of history and hardware,
whose voice hauled onions and sugar,
pig iron and black lace, to remote mountain crossroads—
it's hard to imagine him afraid, as if he were one of us,
of the words of his father.
How strange it must have been for him
to learn that Gabriela Mistral had become a poet
when her lover, who worked for the railroad,
killed himself one night under a barrage of stars.

He was a blue whale,
and unlike the real one, whose baleen
lets in nothing but the red cloud
of krill it lives on, he swallowed everything:
the gray periwinkles he collected from tide pools
and the whole Spanish Civil War, the raw jicama
he loved to douse in a salt bath
and the coal miners' strike of 1947.
When they issued a warrant,
he crossed the Andes on horseback
to Mexico, following almost invisible trails
of smugglers through the forest, and what he remembered
was entering a moist cave
filled with a mountain of cheeses
hidden by miners. There's no way to say this
ironically: he found steam rising

from a volcanic sulfur spring
in a stone basin carved by the water itself,
and he bathed in it, the rock whorls
echoing the delicate chambers of the sea snails he loved
and the labyrinth of an ear
large enough to hear the ocean break on Isla Negra
ten thousand feet below.

He stood behind a podium
reading his poems, and his mouth was enormous—
one could see into the cave of his throat:
paintings of bison on the walls. Incredible
all that erupted from his jaws: goats and handbags,
hieroglyphics and a three-legged stool,
an Easter procession down the one mud road
of a whistle stop, the black seeds of a watermelon
and the monastery outside Madrid
where his poems were copied on white shirts
if they were not too stained with blood,
as there was no paper, but it did not matter
because even paper was in the poems.

It was all cast out of his mouth
until the hall was filled like an ark and the ovation ebbed
and he went out the pneumatic doors
into the night and submerged once more,
an extraterrestrial mammal
encrusted with dingy yellow barnacles
whose songs were sometimes too low for the human ear
but caused tremors
felt in the ribcage and knees, like an earthquake,
even in a quiet village of the Cordilleras
where children were carrying their smudged books
home from school, curious and earnest,
memorizing all the oceans of the world.

Mayflower

Father gave me no warning. He just had me hold
a blaze of daisies, sweet Jesus, sweet
Mary of the emeralds, I didn't even know
I had a brother, or as Sister Margaret
who taught grammar would insist,
had had one. I hadn't asked any questions
when four years before, my stepmother had lumbered
to the hospital and come home a few days later,
alone. Now I didn't even know
if I should unfold the plastic from the stems
before I set them down. It seemed ridiculous
not to, but was that like taking the body
out of its satin wrap?
I saw right away that Robert had lived
for three days. *Robert: they gave you
my name.* They wished it had been me.
No, it *was* me: to them I was nothing,
the whelp of an ex-wife. Father's grief
for you was terrible, but for me was absolute:
no grave to mark it. He didn't even know
it was the loss of me that had gutted his heart.
A blue box kite with a coppery fish
tugged at its twine just over the hill.
I wanted to see it break it, though I knew if it did
it would only fall into a blue gum tree,
splinters for some sparrow's nest.

They put a ship on your stone, Robert,
the *Mayflower*, etched just above your name

as if you were its ocean. That's how Father
wanted to remember you: as one of those Pilgrims
who left everything for a barren shore.
He had left five wives, the last of them your mother—
you never saw how she swirled
her endless brown hair in a bun—
to end harbored with a sixth
on a dead-end street in Fremont, California,
a gingko tree in their backyard
staining the toolshed roof.

Two boys were born on the *Mayflower*
after it had crossed and was at anchor
just off Plymouth, one of them Peregrine,
and the other, stillborn, never given a name.
Think of that. After sixty days on that stinking ship,
surviving on salt cod and vinegar and beer,
Mary Allerton had to walk through water
to get ashore with nothing but a shawl in her arms.
There is no record of what happened to her cradle,
though the sturdy wicker basket of Peregrine White
still exists, one of the only luxuries
allowed onboard, its hood of willow shoots
still shading the bed on its oak rockers.

I mention that, Robert,
because it's what Father would have wanted
you to know. What I want
you to know is this: if it had to be
you or me, your cradle woven of osier
or mine, I'm glad it was me who came ashore
alive and squalling.

The Pilgrims had already fled London and resettled
in tolerant Holland. What roused them to flee again,
to face the weather of the whole Atlantic?
What was it those weavers and coopers feared
in the snug rooms of Amsterdam? Did they see

the face of Satan in the red thread
of a lace maker and the bronze of a bedspread?
Did they find evil in the tarnished shadows
of the face of a woman as plain as Hendrickje,
Rembrandt's wife, painted with an honesty
and tenderness equal to the portraits of his first wife,
the pearls in her hair weighing down her head
as her bare knees entered the stream?
I wish you were here, Robert,
to see her ruby robe barely visible in the background
where it was dropped on the bank.
We could study it together, the folds of warm scarlet,
ocher, and brown that Father never knew.
I can't pretend you knew them either,
but neither can I believe, with him,
that it's something to be proud of,
as if it made you a true American to be alone,
as he was in the end, with hammer and claw
working late in his shed.

Repairing the Hubble Telescope

Floating in God's brain
with nothing but a screwdriver
and a box wrench. With my back to the universe,
I saw the gyroscope I'd come to fix
was the size of the red and gold one I got for Christmas
as a child in Phoenix, the one that made me forget
all my other toys forever. It still amazes me
how something at such a skew can spin so hard
it makes the rest of the world
seem out of whack. That's just how it felt
when the air lock opened and I was out there,
as if all my life I'd been listening to Mozart
on a homemade ham radio, music
measured in megahertz, and now I'd been hurled
into the orchestra pit.

Alexie Leonov was the first, not to walk
in space but to bask in it, cook in it—simmering
in those suits, sweat up to our ankles—
Alexie blurted to his partner on the other side
of the solar panel: *Pavel, look at me, these fucking gloves,
I can't hold the camera, Pavel, I love you,
I don't think I can go back*, and in fact
they overshot the target and almost skidded off
earth's atmosphere entirely and spun out
into interstellar ice, but in the end they simply fell in the snow
of the taiga and waited for helicopters
to find them among the fir trees, stumbling from gravity
like bears drunk on a canyon of berries.

I thought for a moment of Alexie, and of Ed White,
the first American to open
eternity's hatch, and then it was time to get to work.
I could just make out Sumatra and the Malay Peninsula,
the Indian Ocean, before I went under the hood.
Even now people ask me about it
but won't believe me. It wasn't the pure, shimmerless
colors, the anarchic perspective, that changed my life—
it was that moment when I felt exactly
as if I were a kid again, on my driveway in Costa Mesa,
sliding on my back under the chassis.
I was home. The enormous gold foil
rectangles looked like the speakers in my den
as they silently absorbed the sun's white noise.

For once I knew what to do, I lost myself,
and now the whole world can see the Cat's Eye,
a dying star, red and gold, spinning,
and the galaxy Lagoon, full of what the astronomers
call wisps and twisters, star embryos
half a light-year long.

Sitting in my den watching CNN,
squeezing a whole lime in my Diet Coke,
I am homesick
for the only place I ever belonged,
alone with the Hourglass Nebula
and the stars they call blue stragglers,
children wandering on a hillside
among crisscrossing deer trails and mist, almost happy it's so
    late
the search party must be giving up
for the night, the men finishing off the last slug of warmish coffee
from the thermos on the truck's dash,
thinking they know their limits.

The Man Who Could Not Fly

Off work, at the corner of Howard and Spear,
I walk past windows of Parmesan wheels,
ropes of garlic, and cheese from the white oxen
of Tuscany. The bay breeze salts my throat.
My wings carefully folded against my spine,
six layers of gilt-edged feathers
folded each morning like an origami crane
to fit inside my crisp tucked shirt,
begin against my will to ripple, to chafe.
A burning in my shoulder blades spreads
down my ribs as I get closer to the pier.
Pigeons strutting on the plaza give way
to the gulls and forked-tail terns of the sea.
On the sidewalk downtown, men and women
pass me to converge at the edge of the water.
The first ones are already aloft, gliding
toward the Farallon Islands, just visible
in the distance. A woman takes off her coat,
drops it in the street, and the power of the dark
blue pinions that emerge is unbelievable, lifting her
as she cries *klea, klea* to the rasping *krrekk, krrekk*
of a man whose white scapulars beat into the gale.
They have forgotten everything but the lashing wind,
the occasional glint of a fish far below, and the glare
as they dive toward the sun. I take off my shirt,
and my huge, unwieldy wings slowly unfold
and compose themselves. Heavy as armor,
they hang useless and serene. Why must I

come day after day to watch those appalling
plunges, that awful hovering, the ecstatic
shrieking wheels while I stand in the dusk,
my iridescent plumage dignified and rigid?

www.ingramcontent.com/pod-product-compliance
Lightning Source LLC
Chambersburg PA
CBHW031258290426
44109CB00012B/639